AF207255

AFTER THE STORM

BY

REGINA THOMPSON-JENKINS

&

JOHN JENKINS, JR.

Dedication

This book is dedicated in loving memory of our son, Mommy's hero, Tre' Lane. Tre' selflessly sacrificed his life to save the lives of two young ladies when someone chose to randomly shoot into a crowd of people. Tre' was nineteen years old and a full-time college student when he was killed by a senseless act of gun violence that day in 2012. My new purpose, The Tre' Devon Foundation, birthed out of my pain, awards scholarships to graduating high school seniors. Since Tre' inspired multitudes by acting so selflessly, we also honor ordinary citizens that do extraordinary things in the community. By partnering with organizations like the Million Mom March, Everytown, Moms Demand Action, Not in My Neighborhood, Ben's Way, and The Cornelius Boakai Foundation and as a 2018 Everytown Survivor Fellow I share my story and advocate for change, we are well on our way to helping find solutions to combat gun violence and charge legislative officials to do their job with gun control and gun sense laws.

"Growth is necessary for the progress in the journey."
– Regina Thompson-Jenkins

Acknowledgements

First I have to thank God, for his grace and mercy and for keeping me here for a purpose. Thanks go to my husband, John Jenkins, Jr., who is my biggest supporter, my ride-or-die dude for loving me where I am today. I know it wasn't easy journey, but God, I love you for always putting our family first. I appreciate and love you more than you will ever know. It was a long and difficult journey for us. We want to thank our family and friends, who supported and encouraged us along the way. We love you guys. I would like to express my gratitude to the many people who saw us though the process of completing this book, and to all those who provided support, talked things over, read, offered comments, allowed me to quote their remarks, and assisted in the editing, proofreading, and design.

Foreword
By
Councilwoman
Marge Caldwell-Wilson

September 22nd, 2012 will live in my heart and mind forever. As a councilwoman, I had visited the ER on many occasions to comfort families that had lost a child to a shooting. This one was different. This young man died because he chose to save the lives of others. I did not know Tre's parents, Regina and John, until that terrible night in the ER. Here I was in the presence of a couple who had just lost their only child. Memories of my mother flooded my head. She too had lost a child when I was about two years old. I remember watching her in pain, watching her age overnight, and watching her cry uncontrollably.

My heart hurt for Regina and John. I wanted to tell them that time heals, but it really does not. All I could do was offer my support as they dealt with this loss. Regina was inconsolable. John was trying so hard to be strong for her.

Where do they go from here? I thought. How do they not only face burying their child, the victim of a senseless shooting, but face each day for the rest of their lives without him there?

As time went by, I was aware that Regina and John would never overcome their loss, no matter what. I also knew, and in many ways understood, what they were feeling because of what I had witnessed as a child when my mother continually mourned for my sister.

After my mother passed, I wore her locket because I felt it brought me a sense of comfort and closeness. One day I realized that this locket belonged to Regina. She could wear it knowing it belonged to another mother who lost her child. It was my hope that she would accept this gift, and that anytime she wanted to see Tre she could just open up the locket and see his picture.

I know that my mother wouldn't want anyone else to have this locket. She herself walked the path that Regina and John find themselves on. It's their journey now, and a difficult one at that.

The locket will tie me and Regina forever, not only because of where it came from, but also because of what it means to both of us. I believe God works in mysterious ways. He comes to us in ways that we don't always understand. But eventually we realize he is with us.

Regina and John took their grief and made a decision that they would honor Tre's life by helping other young people fulfill their educational goals. Tre would be so proud of them, as I am. They're now walking that difficult path, but they keep going. They have become a voice for parents of shooting victims and for those young people who are struggling with school costs. And they remind our lawmakers that we have to pay attention to the gun violence in our society.

For Regina: Do not judge the bereaved mother. She comes in many forms. She is breathing, but is dying. She may look young, but inside she has become ancient. She smiles, but her heart sobs. She walks, she talks, she cooks, she cleans, and she works. She is, but she is not, all at once. She is here, but part of her is elsewhere for eternity.

For John: One day a son asked his father, "Why do the best die young?"

The father replied, "Let me ask you something. In the meadow, which flowers do you pick?"

The son answered, "The most beautiful ones."

"Exactly," said the father.

Thank you, Tre'. We never met, but you actually introduced me to your parents. I had no idea that night would be the beginning of a friendship I would treasure forever. Tre, Regina, and John, you have touched my life in ways that I can't begin to explain.

Table of Contents

Introduction

To everything there is a season, and a time to every purpose under the heaven: A time to be born, and a time to die; a time to plant, and a time to pluck up that which is planted; A time to kill, and a time to heal; a time to break down, and a time to build up; A time to weep, and a time to laugh; a time to mourn, and a time to dance; A time to cast away stones, and a time to gather stones together; a time to embrace, and a time to refrain from embracing; A time to get, and a time to lose; a time to keep, and a time to cast away; A time to rend, and a time to sew; a time to keep silence, and a time to speak; A time to love, and a time to hate; a time of war, and a time of peace. (Ecclesiastes 3:1-8)

Relentless torment and pain ripped through my life the night my son was killed, as if a funnel from a tornado had discovered my town and eagerly sought to destroy my entire life. Within seconds, the former reality I had grown so accustomed to had been ravaged by a kind of tornado I had never imagined would enter my life. With my world flipped upside down, the cleanup refused to be an easy process.

PSALMS 23

The LORD is my shepherd; I shall not want.

He maketh me to lie down in green pastures:

he leadeth me beside the still waters.

He restoreth my soul:

he leadeth me in the paths of righteousness for
his name's sake.

Yea, though I walk through the valley of the shadow of death,

I will fear no evil: for thou art with me;

thy rod and thy staff they comfort me.

Thou preparest a table before me in the presence
of mine enemies:

thou anointest my head with oil;

my cup runneth over.

Surely goodness and mercy shall follow me all
the days of my life:

and I will dwell in the house of the LORD forever.

Chapter 1:

My Pride and Joy

Tre' burst into this world on the hottest day in July. God blessed me with a son, and I said, "Thank you, God." From the time the doctors placed him in my arms, I was in love with this little person weighing in at seven pounds, five ounces and nineteen inches long. I looked at him and knew he would be an only child. I was so in love; I knew right then I would have the unconditional love only a mother and son would share.

Tre' was introduced to the Lord at an early age by his great-grandmother, affectionately known as mama. Tre' showed talent for playing the drums, starting at age three years old. He received music lessons from the Trenton Community Music School and participated in the Reach for a Note Music Program where he played the keyboards and guitar.

Tre' loved *Barney & Friends*, and I would often sing the theme song to him: "I love you! You love me!" He kept all of his *Barney* VHS tapes, and when I tried to donate them he told me he was saving them for his children. One of my fondness memories of us is when I asked him who the best mommy was in the whole wide world.

He would respond, "You, mom, you."

Then he would ask me who the best son in whole wide world was, and I would respond, "Tre' Devon Lane."

He would say, "Mom, I am your only son."

I would say, "Yes, you are!" Then we would tell each other "I love you."

We made everlasting memories that I will hold in my heart forever. My son was so blessed to have two great men his life on a daily basis: his father, who loved him more than life itself, and his stepfather, my husband John, who loved him so much.

Tre' tried many sports, such as karate, track, golf, tennis, soccer, baseball, and, yes, basketball. He ultimately chose basketball, his passion, and he was good at it. Over the years Tre' played basketball for the Greg Grant 94 Feet League, AAU Teams, and the Red and Black High School team. His love for basketball was another one of his shining moments. I would sit on those bleachers all over again if only I could see him play one more time. You couldn't tell #23 anything, and he knew his mother would be always sitting on those bleachers coaching and cheering him on at every single game. Tre' and I used to watch the basketball games of our favorite team the Chicago Bulls on television as he sat glued to the TV as he admired his favorite player #23, Michael Jordan. I used to listen to him run off all of the stats about his favorite player. He knew everything about that team. On Sundays our house was filled with excitement, loud sounds, and fun with plenty of snacks. Tre' and I were true diehard Philadelphia Eagles fans and my husband is a fan of the Dallas Cowboys.

Lovingly, I often reminded him of the nine months of sickness and four days of labor when he needed it, and he used to say, "I know, Mom; you told me this story a million times." As Tre' matured into a young man, he grew to the lanky stature of

6'4", and he stood out in a room. He was very popular among the girls, a chick magnet for sure. Oh yes, he loved the girls, but his favorite girl was his mother. She was his everything, and he was her everything. Tre' was affectionately known around town for his smile and those dimples. He always had a kind word to say about everybody. Tre' was very respectful to everyone he encountered. It was his nature.

During his high school years he started out in private school and then transferred to public school by his own choice with some careful consideration from my husband and me. He made the transition to his new school smoothly. He always had great instincts with the foundation of being raised right and could adjust to any situation while maintaining his own morals and values that were taught by his role model, his mother. His weakest subject was math, which he excelled at with the help of a tutor. He was a member of the choir and the basketball team. He went on to graduate in 2011. He was so proud on that day as he walked across the stage knowing his family was cheering him on in the audience. I was bursting inside with pride, joy, and tears. All of my hard work and sacrifices were about to pay off. He looked at me as he accepted his diploma and nodded his head as if to say "I did it, Mom! I did it!!" I gave him the thumbs up, tears of joy streamed down my face.

Tre' was a warm person and had a gentle heart. I taught him the importance of giving back to the less fortunate; he spent many hours volunteering in the community. Even though he was an only child, he was not a selfish person. Tre' was involved in many extracurricular activities such as the Mercer County Smile—Gear Up program for seven years, which gears students toward college. At the time of his death he was enrolled at Mercer County Community College pursuing a degree in social work. After MCCC his plan was to transfer to William Patterson University, where he planned to get his degree as a social worker because he enjoyed helping people. He had received his SORA certification, and he was extremely proud of this accomplishment.

Tre' had a strong work ethic and was employed as a security guard while working his way through school. My son did everything I asked of him: he graduated from high school, he went to college, and he worked. He was a productive citizen of society. He was a great son! I was so proud of him, and everyone around me knew it, but more important, I made sure he knew it.

With his spoiled butt!

My son, I don't know why God made you a hero and one of his angels on that fatal autumn day. All I know is that my heart is broken, and my family is shattered. It has been hard for me to go on without you because you were such a big part of my world. Everything revolved around God, you, and our family, and right now, baby, my heart is broken; my spirit, my mind can barely think straight; my heart aches for you and your presence. I am trying to wrap my head around all of this and make sense of it.

All I get is, why you? Why you?

I know you are all right; you are with God, Mama, and the rest of the family. My son, you will always be my hero! Your strength, your courage, your true character shone on that day. All of the things I instilled in you shone, and for that I am so proud to be your mother. Rest in peace, my son, for you made

Mommy proud! I love you, Tre', with all of my being and every breath in my body. Then we who are alive and remain shall be caught up together with them in the clouds to meet the Lord in the air, and so shall we ever be with the Lord.

For the Lord Himself shall descend from heaven with a shout, with the voice of the archangel and the trump of God, and the dead in Christ will rise first. 1 Thessalonians 4: 16–17

Chapter 2:

— ❖ —

Grief

Have you ever noticed that grief is like a thief in the night? It comes to steal joy and rob your peace, and it lingers like halitosis. No one asks for it or prays for it, and it has the audacity to approach you while you are minding your own business in life. Then—*bam!* It knocks vehemently on your door. It's comparable to unwelcomed constipation, a superglue of pain, and the unhappy vacation place all in one.

There are many individuals who have lost precious loved ones: sisters, brothers, moms, dads, aunts, uncles, confidants, coworkers, grandparents, neighbors, sons, daughters, nieces, and nephews. We have all suffered grief. We hurt. Some feel cheated. Grief is not prejudiced. It affects people of all ages, creed, color, and socioeconomic status.

No one ever gets out of bed and says, "Hey, where's my friend, grief?" After a traumatic accident, grief diligently finds you when you are vulnerable, frail, and unprepared. It's quite clearly the beast that won't quit until you make some healthy decisions, and have some healthy conversations like I did.

My husband gave me a little powerful book on grief and its ramifications. The book indicated that grief was a journey that moved over terrain over territories and regions. I have found this to be true, and I know the simplest definition of grief is deep sorrow.

I am a book junkie, and I have derived strength from another book that filled me with comfort during my time of sorrow, helped me feel a sense of peace and gave me hope. There were prayers that expressed the pain of my heart and didn't require me to speak a word. Some prayers reminded me of the need to take it one day at a time and others spoke to my brokenness offering me courage for each day. These prayers have a fullness of riches that I have needed at such broken and emotionally devastated periods in my life.

I have witnessed the type of grief that can alter one's appearance, appetite, sleep, posture, employment status, and ultimately longevity. I have experienced many faces of grief. If unmanaged, grief can make a prince look like a frog in a relatively short period of time. The true damage is to the heart, mind, and emotions as it sucks at and shakes the very core of our existence.

It feels like an emotional millstone hanging from your neck to the floor. You can scream at grief and say, "Get out of here!" You can kick it and punch it. It is stubborn and won't move an inch. It knows that you have to matriculate through the university of its stages.

But thou, O LORD, art a shield for me; my glory, and the lifter up of mine head. Psalms 3:3

Processing a love one's death will come in stages and in no particular order. There is much research that suggests there are seven stages of grief.

SHOCK AND DENIAL

You will probably react to learning of the loss with numbed disbelief. You may deny the reality of the loss of someone you love at some level to avoid the pain. Shock provides emotional protection from being overwhelmed all at once. This may last for weeks.

PAIN AND GUILT

As the shock wears off, it is replaced with the suffering of unbelievable pain. Although excruciating and almost unbearable, it is important that you experience the pain fully and not hide it, avoid it, or escape from it with alcohol or drugs. You may have guilty feelings or remorse over things you did or didn't do with your loved one. Life feels chaotic and scary during this phase.

ANGER AND BARGAINING

Frustration gives way to anger, and you may lash out and lay unwarranted blame for the death on someone else. Please, try to control this, as permanent damage to your relationships may result. This is a time for the release of bottled-up emotions.

You may rail against fate, questioning, "Why me?" You may also try to bargain in vain with the Powers That Be for a way out of your despair (Like, I will never drink again if you just bring my loved one back).

DEPRESSION, REFLECTION, AND LONELINESS

Just when your friends may think you should be getting on with your life, a long period of sad reflection will likely overtake you.

This is a normal stage of grief, so do not be "talked out of it" by well-meaning outsiders. Encouragement from others is not helpful to you during this stage of grief. It might just make you mad.

During this time, you finally realize the true magnitude of you loss, and it depresses you. You may isolate yourself on purpose, reflect on things you did with your lost one, and focus on memories of the past. You may sense feelings of emptiness or despair.

THE UPWARD TURN

As you start to adjust to life without your dear one, your life becomes a little calmer and more organized. Your physical symptoms lessen, and your depression begins to lift slightly.

RECONSTRUCTION AND WORKING THROUGH

As you become more functional, your mind starts working again, and you will find yourself seeking realistic solutions to problems posed by life without your loved one. You will start to work on practical and financial problems and reconstructing yourself and your life without them.

ACCEPTANCE AND HOPE

During the last of the seven stages in this grief model, you learn to accept and deal with the reality of your situation. Acceptance does not mean instant happiness. Given the pain and turmoil you have experienced, you can never return to the carefree, untroubled version of you who existed before this tragedy. However, you will find a way forward.

You will start to look ahead and actually plan things for the future. Eventually, you will be able to think about your lost loved one without pain. There will be sadness, yes, but the wrenching pain will be gone. You will once again anticipate some good times to come and, yes, even find joy again in the experience of living.

In the finale of grief, I have learned that what doesn't kill you has the potential to make you stronger, wiser, more mature, and ultimately better. The sun will shine on you, and you will see brighter days ahead. Don't give up. Just keep on pushing.

Weeping may endure for a night but joy cometh in the morning. Psalms 30:5

Chapter 3:

Premonition

At first, I never gave a second thought to the word *premonition*. Most view it as a childish belief belonging to the world of the few who have faith and indulged in everything make-believe. It's defined as a strong feeling something is about to happen, especially something unpleasant.

Have you ever questioned yourself when visiting a restaurant when you knew for a fact that you'd never visited it before in your entire life? Before entering the restaurant, you could swear you already knew exactly what was on the menu or even knew that the wallpaper would be monochromatic shades of blue. Or perhaps you knew what you would eat before asking yourself?

It's similar to meeting a perfect stranger and knowing verbatim the next words they will utter before they open their mouth and say one word. Frightening, isn't it?

Before my grandmother passed, I had a dream about how her entire funeral would take place: how she would be laid to rest in the soft earth in her crisp, white suit, down to the off-white clothes her loved ones would be wearing. Being the eldest grandchild, I knew I would have to be the one to speak.

Prior to her death, all I could feel was deafening guilt for dreaming such disturbing visions. However, after she passed on July 4th, gaining her own sort of independence, her funeral went exactly the way I had dreamed.

My world crumbled the day she died. Our relationship was an unbreakable bond because she had practically made me the woman I am today. Depression quickly overtook me as her death took an immense toll on my life. Unfortunately, I never had the opportunity to grieve the same way my loved ones were able to due to the constant reminder that I would have to fill her shoes and be there for my family.

Ever since I was young, I aspired to be the beautiful, graceful, and spiritual woman she was. I admired the way she always put God and her independence first all the way up to the minute she died. I believe my biggest mistake in recovering from her death, without question, was never receiving proper grief counseling.

When it came to Tre's death, I received a strange, unsettling dream a couple of days before. My grandmother came to me, her features laced with worry as she repeatedly told me Tre' had been shot and I needed to get to the hospital. In the dream, I dressed myself in world-record time and raced to my truck, which had just been towed. A very real panic coursed through my system as I darted across the street toward the parking lot of the hospital. My eyes were set on the hospital. But every time I put one foot in front of me, it was as if I weren't moving an inch, which caused my blood pressure to skyrocket.

I woke up abruptly, seconds before I could see the end result of my dream.

Now that I think about it, I'd had similar dreams before then, dreams where I viewed my son in a casket with a black suit, white shirt, and a royal blue tie. Just like with my grand-mother, I felt utterly guilt ridden for dreaming of something so morbid. I never assumed it was a premonition.

From the time that our children enter the world, our job as parents is to protect them from harm's way. I purposely didn't warn my son about my dream for the sole reason that I didn't want to frighten him. At the time, I didn't see it as a crucial piece of information.

However, from then on I asked him to come home early every night, and he obliged until the Friday night when he wanted to hang out with family. I was hesitant to let him leave, remembering the warning my grandmother had sent me in my dream. But against my better judgment, I gave him the benefit of being a regular teen. I figured he didn't deserve such an overprotective mom, as he was a great kid. As a full-time college student with a part-time job as a security guard, he gave me no reason to worry.

I remember it clearly, like it was yesterday. I kissed my son and told him I loved him for the last time that night without realizing it was my final goodbye. The moment he stepped out the front door my stomach flipped, so I checked up on him at exactly 9:01 p.m., asking him to be careful that night.

He texted back, *Alright, Mom, I love you!*

I attempted to drift off to sleep but found myself unable to let my brain shut down for a few hours. I was wracked with worry for a reason unknown to me at the time.

I asked my husband to check to see if Tre' were home yet, only for him to return to tell me Tre's room was empty. My heart dropped when his words hit my ears, and anxiety shot through my body as my husband tried to console me. I talked myself out of calling my son, sure that I was simply overreacting.

I'll never forget the deafening rings of the phone that night. I remember a pit in my stomach forming when my mother called at 1:00 a.m., screaming frantically in the phone.

"Gina, go to the hospital. Tre' was shot."

The words etched themselves into my memory. My heart dropped as an overwhelming sense of nausea struck me.

I remember shooting out of bed and dressing myself in fifteen seconds. My emotions flew as I sat in the car, unable to help my son in any way at that moment. The sense of not knowing whether or not your child is close to death is one I wouldn't wish upon anyone.

"Please God, fix my baby!" I sent millions of prayers to the sky, hoping He would hear at least just one.

From the second I burst through the hospital doors, thick tension sat in the air. My family was waiting for me solemnly with terrified expressions plastered on their faces. I couldn't imagine my features appeared much different.

I was quickly informed I couldn't see him as he had already been rushed to surgery. As I waited, two girls approached me, explaining how Tre's heroic actions had saved their lives, and if it weren't for him, they would most likely be in his place.

For five and a half hours we waited anxiously with friends and family. When they finally came out to escort my husband and me, a sliver of hope filled my heart. We both thought they were leading us to see my son, whom we assumed was in recovery. However, we were asked to hold up in a holding room to await a doctor who wouldn't show for what seemed like an eternity, though in reality, it was only a few minutes. My nerves and a nauseous stomach sent me to the lady's room too many times to count. The last time I returned from the restroom, the doctor and a few nurses were waiting for me. Their expressions made my heart stop, instantly shattering my faith.

With very little hope, I asked, "Can I see my son now?"

The doctor hesitated before saying, "I am so sorry, ma'am."

"Sorry about what?" My voice cracked, and my eyes began to burn.

"I am so sorry. We did all that we could, but your son didn't make it."

I remember him going on to say that Tre' was a fighter and that during surgery he had bled out on the table. Everything he said after that sounded eerily similar to the robot teacher in the classic Charlie Brown cartoon specials. My brain went numb, and I stumbled back a bit in shock. I screamed at the top of my lungs, and my body went into spastic convulsions of horror and tears. My family could hear me wailing from the waiting room.

I vaguely remember being helped across the room, where I fainted. My soul was unwilling to take on any more of the nightmare unfolding before my eyes.

After regaining consciousness, I begged my husband to tell me it was just a dream. But when I saw I was surrounded by family, the news was confirmed. My worst nightmare had come true. But I couldn't accept it. My brain wouldn't allow me to believe that this was my reality.

I had to see my son. This couldn't be he to whom the doctor was referring. I needed to see if that were really my son in the morgue.

Making my way to identify his body felt like a five-mile trek where I constantly had to remind myself to breathe.

When we finally arrived at the door, I sent my husband in first. All I could see was a lifeless body resting on a stainless-steel table wrapped in a harsh-looking black body bag.

I called out, "Is it Tre'?" My husband didn't respond. "Answer me! Is it Tre'?"

By the look of horror on my husband's face and the tears that began to stream down his cheeks, I knew it was our son's body. So, I slowly walked over to the table to see for myself.

My confirmation was complete. I bent down, shaking uncontrollably, to kiss my lifeless son as tears fell down my face. All I could do was cry, cry, and cry even more to a point where I was shocked I hadn't run out of tears. My tears seemed endless. Grief can be an extremely lonely and terrifying place. Confusion and disbelief are all a part of it. We had tried so hard to protect our son for nineteen years.

For nineteen years we loved him, nourished him, and pushed him to do his best. Now nineteen years' worth of love was gone, taken away with by one heartless decision randomly made by a sociopathic monster. Senseless violence had robbed our beloved son of life and a future.

After the longest day I had ever experienced, my husband took me home, both of us silent the whole way there. I remember taking a long, hot shower and sobbing for at least an hour. My husband had to come upstairs to help me get out the shower because my body was so numb. I couldn't feel anything.

I fell into my husband's arms and asked him, "Why my baby? What did we do to deserve this? What did Tre' do to deserve this?"

I didn't understand; my son didn't live the street life. He was sheltered. Who would want to hurt my son?

The days leading up to the funeral were difficult, but there were lots of people stopping by the house and calling each day.

But then once the funeral was over and Tre' was buried in the cemetery, everyone stopped visiting our house. The cards stopped coming in, and no more meals were being delivered. My husband and I looked at each other, realizing that the real work of grieving was about to begin.

But we remembered the Word of God in Jeremiah 31:13, where the Lord says, "I will turn their mourning into joy, I will comfort them, and give them gladness for sorrow."

We had been avoiding our home and the memories it held since the death of our son because we simply couldn't face the reality of the loss. I constantly wondered about the "what if's." What could I have done differently that night? It was as if I knew nothing. As a parent, your first instinct is to protect our children at any cost. All I ever yearned to do was protect my baby from harm's way. I knew I couldn't always keep him safe twenty-four hours a day; that was impossible. But still I wanted to try. I often prayed and asked God why my baby had to die. I wondered what I had done that was so terrible that God would punish me by taking my only child. My faith was being shaken, and I was subconsciously angry with God even though I never said it out loud.

Chapter 4:

— ❖ —

Broken

In 3.3 seconds my life was flipped upside down. I felt like a tornado funnel blew into my town and let out a roar! "Children are a gift from the Lord" (Psalms 127:3). No parent is ever prepared to deal with the loss a child.

I will not leave you comfortless: I will come to you. John: 14:18

In my darkest hour, I needed my faith because I didn't understand the loss of my baby. I prayed a lot and ask God why?

Depression quickly set in with me. I wanted to jump off the Verrazano Bridge; I simply didn't want to live. I wasn't eating or sleeping. I felt like I just existed. But for what? Each day that passed felt like eternity without my baby. If I have cried one tear, I have cried a million tears since my son has been gone. Each tear represents the fear of losing the memories I have of him in my heart. The pain I felt when a tear fell was like an eighteen-wheeler Mack truck rolling back and forth over me.

I know that if I look up in the sky, the stars will shine bright, and I envision his face and hope that he will give me a sign that he is missing me too.

I forced myself out of bed each day and managed to go through the motions, almost as though I were having an out-of-body experience watching myself on a movie screen. I took a leave of absence from my job and really didn't know when I was going back to work. I really didn't care. My entire day-to-day routine was drastically altered. I had to write everything down: bills to be paid, due dates, medical appointments, and the rest. I couldn't remember things or focus on anything. For months I couldn't drive myself anywhere.

I realized that I couldn't begin the long, hard journey of healing without professional help. The doctor prescribed some pills, but I didn't see the point in taking them because my problem would still be there once the effects of the pills wore off. My son would still be dead and beyond my reach. The pills were only a temporary Band-Aid, and I could have very easily become addicted to their numbing effect. That was not the type of life I wanted to live.

This drug-free period of mourning worked for me. But I advise every individual facing such depression to seek their doctor's advice. Sometimes we think we don't need to talk to anyone. But it is a mistake to think that we can do it all on our own. I needed to lie on the doctor's couch and talk about my feelings, or else I would have wound up lying in a coffin. My heart was hurting, and I didn't know how to fix it. There was a hole in my heart that made everything else in life seem empty.

Don't get me wrong. I had plenty of support. The people around me really didn't grieve the same way I was grieving. Neither did anyone understand my unique experience of this tragic loss. How could they? Family and friends all went back to work eventually. Alone, I was left to pick up the pieces. My husband would make me get out bed. I just wanted to roll over and pull the sheets up over my head. Without Tre', it seemed like I no longer had any reason to get out bed.

There were days when my husband just wanted me to feel the sun on my face. I just couldn't deal with people or crowds staring at me, saying, "I am so sorry about your son," or, "My condolences on the loss of your son." It made it all too real and in my face for me to deal with. The first year after Tre's death, I walked around numbly, in a fog, almost as if the experience weren't real, a bad dream. The second year was worse. The numbness began to wear off. Then it was all too real. Tears flowed constantly, so much that my eyes remained swollen day after day. Every night I would have to place a cold compress on my eyes to soothe them. My entire body was in immense, agonizing pain.

Each year I felt more of the numbness wearing off. My feelings of desolation became progressively worse, more crippling than the year before. I was absolutely unable to bear the weight of this loss. I wanted the pain and the rollercoaster of emotions to stop. My mind was always thinking about something: the funeral, the memories, the should haves, the could haves, and the would haves. Too often, this hyper-thought activity threatened to propel me from a condition of being dazed to a full comatose state. That is when I was lead to read the "Serenity Prayer" over and over again:

God grant me the serenity

to accept the things, I cannot change;

courage to change the things I can;

and wisdom to know the difference.

Living one day at a time;

enjoying one moment at a time;

accepting hardships as the pathway to peace;

taking, as He did, this sinful world

as it is, not as I would have it; trusting that He will make all things right if I surrender to His Will; that I may be reasonably happy in this life and supremely happy with Him

forever in the next. Amen.

I live my life one day at a time. When I lost the love of my life as a mother, it made me love less across the board. It is hard for me to get close to people now without some fear that I will lose them. I know we all have to go one day or another.

But for me the loss is even more pronounced. I don't go to funerals except for immediate family, and I never go up to view the body. This rule is for my own sanity. We have to do what is best for our individual mental health. A year after my son died, my husband's daughter had a baby. I couldn't pick up the baby without memories of my own child overwhelmingly flooding my heart, mind, and soul. I just didn't want to see that baby or any other baby. I wasn't ready! You don't lose a child without everything in your life changing. I was broken and didn't know how to continue on with my life.

The Lord is close to the brokenhearted and saves those who are crushed in spirit. Psalm 34:18

I encountered many trials while on this journey, such as going into my son's room. It was very hard for me to do. My mind always protects me until I seem ready, but my heart deals with each test differently. Recovery is an altogether unpredictable process.

Five months into it marked the time for me to go into Tre's room. So, I decided to send my husband to the store. I knew it was going to take him some time because I gave him a list of groceries that I really didn't need. Sitting on the side of my bed wondering how to approach this mountain, I began sweating as my feet dangled off the side of the bed, swinging back and forth. Then I received a text message from my auntie: *"Perfect love cast out fear—I John 4:18."* She went on to say that the perfect love I had for my son would cast out any doubts I was having about my recovery.

I texted back, "Auntie, how did you know I was going into his room?" She said God told her to send that verse to me. I walked down the hallway slowly with tears flowing, each tear larger and heavier than the last. I put my hand on the doorknob and took a deep breath.

Finally, I opened the door to Tre's room. The air in the room was stifling. It took my breath away. I instantly hyperventilated. I picked up his pillow and smelled it. It smelled like him. I let out a blood-curdling scream. If the window had been open, someone outside would have called the police thinking I was in danger. The sobbing continued as I walked around the room. I touched everything: his hairbrush, his trophies, and even his security guard uniform. He had worn it the night before, and it still smelled like him. My son kept every card I ever gave him. I read all of them. Each tear fell harder than the last. His room was exactly as he left it. Going into his room brought back so many memories. Tre' had occupied the same room since he was eighteen months old, just a toddler.

In that moment, the realization hit me. My son was never

coming back! I dropped to my knees and began to cry uncontrollably while holding his pillow. Taking one last look around the room, as if it were going to be my last time going in there, I stood in the doorway with my trembling hand on the doorknob. Enormous tears were falling from my eyes. Then I closed the door, ran down the hallway to my bedroom, and fell across my bed. As I lay there, collapsed, I heard the front door open. It was my husband returning from the store. I hurriedly got a tissue and tried to wipe away my tears. But when he saw me, he instantly knew.

He asked, "You went in his room?"

I said, "Yes."

He put his arms around me, and we cried together. I thought I was brave enough to go in there. But looking back, emotionally, I wasn't ready. I knew that a future without my son looked very bleak for me.

For thus says the Lord, "As a mother comforts her child, so I will comfort you. Isaiah 66:12-13

The next Sunday, I awoke and told my husband I needed to go to church. So, we went. The praise and worship music were amazing. I was clapping my hands and patting my feet to the rhythm of the beat. Then the pastor rose up in the pulpit and started to preach about a woman in the bible who went to God in prayer because her son was dying.

She asked, "God, why would you give me this child and then take him away from me?"

I broke down in the church. Everyone was staring at me as if to inquire, "What's wrong with her?"

Therefore, the pastor brought my husband and me to the altar for prayer and asked me if she could share with the congregation why I was so emotional. I said yes! The congregation embraced us with many healing hugs. We had found a church home where we could renew our faith in God.

Chapter 5:

The Journey

Have you ever gotten into your car and arrived at your destination, but you didn't remember driving the route, how you got there, or what you remember along the way? That's how I would describe grief.

By now, the spirit of grief and I have gotten to know each other really well. So here we were left to pick up the pieces, but I didn't know how to do that. I could barely get out of the bed in the morning. One thing my husband did not allow me was to stay in bed. He would get me out of the house to focus on something else just for a few hours.

Notice, I said "a few hours." Your grief will always be in on your mind or in the forefront of it. There were days I had to convince my husband that I just wanted to be left alone and stay in my bed. My husband was very concerned and told my primary doctor. She suggested that I seek a professional psychologist. I met with the doctor, and she had experienced loss herself. After she evaluated me, she recommend that I needed more treatment in addition to her office visits. She said she would prescribe me some pills; she said it would help me sleep and assist with anxiety.

I asked, "Will it bring my son back?"

She said soberly, "Unfortunately, no."

I told her that at the end of the day it didn't matter how many pills I took; it wouldn't take away my pain. The hole in my heart was brilliantly still there. She recommended that I attend an out-patient facility for my depression. I agreed even though I had suicidal thoughts. After leaving her office, I told my husband, "I am not taking the pills."

My first day at this outpatient facility, I felt confused and overwhelmed. I wasn't crazy. I had lost my only child, and I was grieving. This facility had a mix of people; there were suicidal, drug- and alcohol-addicted people and ones with mental disorders. The counselors there were very nice, and I was shown around the facility. I kind of stayed to myself the first day. I remember coming home and telling my husband, "That place isn't for me. I feel like they think I am crazy or something."

Philippians 4:13

He said, "Give it one try more, and if you don't feel comfortable, you won't have to go back. We will find something else for you."

I went back the next day, and each day I had to sign up for the sessions I wanted to be in for the day. I attended this facility three days a week for almost three months. I remember attending art therapy on the second day there. I went to the session, and I felt connected. It awakened something in me. I learned how to express my grief through art.

Looking at the board, I saw there wasn't a session for grief, so I asked the counselor why. The very next day I looked up, and there was a session for grief. Gandhi said it best, "Be the change you wish to see in the world." I and so many other people signed up for the session. I remember saying, "Wow."

For I know the thoughts that I think toward you, saith the Lord, thoughts of peace, and not of evil, to give you an expected end. Jeremiah 29:11

In a group session, people tend to share out. Some of them shared that they had a loss that put them on the path to their spiraling road to drug and alcohol addiction. They expressed the fact that they never received help for their loss.

There hath no temptation taken you but such as is common to man: but God is faithful, who will not suffer you to be tempted above that ye are able; but will with the temptation also make a way of escape, that you may be able to bear it. 1 Corinthians 10:1

After leaving that session, I reflected that I could have easily been one of those people who was addicted to drugs or alcohol. That could have been me!

For the grace of God there go I.

But the God of all grace, who hath called us unto his eternal glory by Christ Jesus, after that ye have suffered a while, make you perfect, stablish, strengthen, settle you. 1Peter 5:10

Journaling has become cathartic for me. I highly advise you to express your feelings on paper when you don't or can't talk to someone. I still attended my grief sessions with Compassionate Friends as well. I really relate to the people in this group because everyone there has experienced the loss of a child. They knew the pain I was going through, and I knew what they were feeling. As time went on, I took on somewhat of a leadership role in the group from writing the newsletter to facilitating the monthly meeting. I surprised myself at times. Still working on rebuilding my faith, I continued to go to church.

But let him ask in faith, nothing wavering. For he that wavereth is like a wave of the sea driven and tossed. James 1:6

The church played an important role in getting my faith back and having a relationship with God again.

Who is he that overcometh the world, but he that believeth that Jesus is the son of God. 1 John 5:5

One day while we were attending church, the pastor preached on forgiveness. I turned to my husband and said, "You know I am not there yet."

He said, "I know, babe." So after going to church Sunday after Sunday, I learned a few things. Forgiveness is not for the other person; it's for me. It's for you. I remember meeting another mother who had lost her son roughly twenty years before. I remember her telling the story of how she was in the grocery store and one of the killers who murdered her son tapped her on the shoulder while she was in line to pay for her items. I asked her what she did, and she told me that he startled her.

The guy said to her, "I want to apologize to you and ask you for your forgiveness."

I asked her, "What did you say?"

She said, "I forgave him."

I told her I wasn't ready to forgive the person who took my son's life. That's when she went on to say forgiveness was for her, not him. That definitely was food for thought.

Ye have not chosen me, but I chose you. John 15:16

In the journey of grieving I met one of the girls whom my son saved that night. She came up to me and gave me a big hug; no conversation was exchanged. It felt like a weight was lifted off of her shoulders. After the long hug, I told her that my son sacrificed his life so she could live, and I needed her to do something with her life to make it meaningful and pay it forward.

Let us not be weary in well doing: for in due season we shall reap, if we faint not. Galatians 6:9-10

On my journey, I have met many wonderful people who are hurting but looking for courage to face the loss. I remember reaching out to a woman at a vigil at a college-sponsored event for our children. I reached out to greet this woman; her heart was touched, and we have been constant friends ever since. She has added healing into my life, and I believe I have been a strength to her. We meet monthly just to fellowship, share, and motivate each other. This is a beautiful thing.

As I continued my journey, I made a note to myself: Be patient with yourself.

The Lord gave, and the Lord has taken away; blessed be the name of the Lord. Job 1:21

Grief tends to last longer than most people assume it will. It's a process laced with hardships that lead you through an unexpected journey. Grief is a path that few want to take, even when it is necessary. We know that death is inevitable. God said everyone has an expiration date. There's no point in attempting to avoid the unpleasant events in life. In all honesty, almost anything can trigger the pain that results in tears: a special picture, a song, or even a certain smell.

One day I was driving, and my son's favorite song came on the radio. I was struck with grief. I began to weep uncontrollably. I pulled over to regain my composure and wipe my tears away. Once the song ended, I dried my tears and continued on my way.

This still happens more times than I care to count.

I genuinely thought I was slowly losing my mind because, at any given moment, I would crumble without warning. However, I constantly reminded myself to be patient and let God do His work.

I ran across a quote on Facebook one day. I read it over and over again: "Grief is forever, it is a journey that will have its highs and lows at some point. Expect the unexpected."

Trying to put my life back together hasn't been easy for us. Just trying to find reasons to live is a daily struggle. I force myself to get out of bed daily. But for what? My husband takes me out of the house each day whether for a simple walk or a trip to the grocery store. He just wants me on my feet. Usually, by the time we return to the house, it's already dark and time for bed. (Notice how I didn't say time for sleep?) I can't sleep, and sleeplessness only forces me into a state of sleep deprivation where I am left feeling completely exhausted.

In my effort to deal with this traumatic loss, I started to journal, writing all of my thoughts, the good, the bad, and the ugly. I journaled because it allowed me to express the way I felt at the time, clearly, on paper in black and white. This provided a way for me to confront my feelings. It allowed me to scream, rant, rave, and cry through my writing. Did it help? Yes, but only for a moment. Journaling was absolutely therapeutic for me. Pen and paper gave me a place where I could feel safe in my own mind. I could say what I wanted to say, and no one could judge me or pity me. I continuously scribbled down every emotion, every thought, and every memory of my precious son that happened to cycle through my brain.

The process of grief can be devastating for anyone going through the different stages. No one experiences the stages of grief in any particular order. There are no rules governing the process of mourning. It's quite similar to being on a roller coaster. Emotions can and will flare at any moment, and there's nothing you can do to stop the tears.

When going through such struggles in life, I vehemently suggest postponing major life decisions if possible. Wait until a time when your mind is calm and clear before deciding such things as whether to sell your house or change your job. During my first year of grieving, I was completely numb with shock. I was walking around in a fog, not noticing the people around me and constantly in my own little world. I couldn't remember anything, and reality quickly seemed to slip from my grasp. I had to write down every bill and appointment just so I could remember them. I still couldn't process what had happened to my precious, only baby. Everything he could've been in the future constantly filled my thoughts.

My grief therapist told me not to make any major life-altering decisions at that point in my life. It seemed to be simple advice to follow, but all I wanted to do was move into a new house where I wasn't haunted by the looming memories of my son. The house I was currently living in was no longer a home without the love and laughter that had radiated from my son.

Fortunately, I took the advice of the experts, and I waited three whole years to start looking for a new house. Each person is different and therefore grieves differently. Doing what is best for you and seeking professional advice before making any big decisions can speed your recovery drastically. It is one of the reasons why I love counseling. It introduces you to a new world of thinking by a trained, objective professional. Sometimes we need conversations outside of our friends and family. We can show a greater side of vulnerability. We need to talk with some-one who can dig deeply inside our emotions to help us work out the emotional kinks.

My husband and I are all too often reminded about special holidays that constantly bring back the pain and suffering. The fact that Tre' died two months before the Thanksgiving and Christmas holiday season has made me despise the holidays. Those were the worst ninety days of my life.

I remember getting up on Thanksgiving morning and going down to the kitchen to prepare the ingredients required to make sweet potato pie. But for the life of me I couldn't remember the recipe. Frustrated, all I wanted to do was bake for Tre'. I had taught Tre' how to bake a sweet potato pie. The fond memory of my son and me cooking together flashed through my mind, and I was suddenly riddled with a wave of tears. My husband wrapped me in his arms and told me I didn't need to bake that year. Later that day, we visited Tre' at the cemetery, which only further ruined my day, sending me into another whirlwind of sobs.

Christmas was around the corner, and the closer it came, the more anxious I became. I had a flashback to 2011 when my son was still alive and thriving. I had the flu, and I was lying on the couch. But Tre' insisted that we put a tree up. He even offered to decorate it all by himself. I reluctantly agreed and groggily got dressed to buy the tree he had yearned for so passionately. I clearly remember Tre' picking out the biggest tree on the lot. It was so enormous that we had to take it back twice to get it sized. I remember him setting up the train around it and decorating the branches with sparkling ornaments and lights.

Christmas tends to be a holiday I would rather avoid because my son absolutely adored it. Celebrating seemed so unfair since Tre' couldn't experience it with us any longer. I'm well aware that I started to become a Debbie Downer to everyone around me. I simply was just not in the mood to be around people at that time. On Tre's birthday, my family visited the cemetery. We released balloons filled with messages of love. The party we held for my son brought us to tears of happiness and sadness as we shared our memories.

When your loved one dies, the grief can be paralyzing. In our case, it was our one and only son. And the aftermath dragged our hitherto average lives into a spiraling, crumbling world of despair. But through the support from loved ones, we fought hard every day to carry on with our lives, if not for ourselves, then for Tre'.

Chapter 6:

❖

Men Cry in the Dark

As with most couples, my husband and I take each other for granted in the relationship, and complacency becomes the norm. I remember my wedding day so vividly: the butterflies and the love I felt going into that day. I thought the feelings I felt on that day would last forever and that would be enough to make our marriage last. I quickly learned that the wedding was just for that day and the marriage is for a lifetime. The real work begins after the honeymoon with sacrifices and compromising. There was no more "I" but "we."

Don't get me wrong. I love my husband, and I know he loves me, but when a tragedy strikes it can destroy the love, respect, and the relationship that you have built in an instant. When tragedy struck our household it quickly shifted back to " I." It was no longer the institution of "us."

"I am grieving; I can't be your wife right now whatever that entails," I would tell him.

It seemed as if God were testing me to see how we were dealing with this as a couple. (That's a key word, "couple.") I was failing the test. I couldn't think about my marriage at a time when my whole world had been shaken upside down and inside out. My husband couldn't understand the magnitude of the pain and devastation of my grief. During this season, I ate grief for breakfast, lunch, and dinner. My feelings were real and coupled with real pain. As a mother, the word "I" came into our relationship a lot during my grieving process. I felt I had to be selfish to get through this difficult time. By this time, grief and I had intertwined.

There were times I knew it was wrong, but I didn't care because I had to take care of me. I didn't care about myself or my marriage. As time went on my world became even darker, and I didn't want to be around my husband, fearful he would pressure me to be his wife again when I wasn't ready.

Selfishly not acknowledging his feelings at the time, I gave him several options, none of them viable. When I look back, I see I had a mental meltdown. I told him, "You can walk out the door, and I am willing to give you a divorce." The second option was that I was willing to give him a pass to cheat because I knew I couldn't be the woman he needed me to be for him as his wife.

Looking back, I know cheating should never be a viable option in a marriage, and no man should ever get a pass. I am truly glad that God allowed me to be married to the man that I am.

The first thing he did was take my hand, and then he said to me, "I am not going anywhere, and we will not be getting a divorce." The next thing was, "I don't have to cheat. I married the woman of my dreams, and I am off the market." He said patience was a virtue, God got us, and we would get through this together.

My tears rolled down my face; each tear tasted saltier than the next. He gently wiped away my tears. God puts the right people in your life for reason or a season. In that moment, I knew what being in love really meant and that our vows were for better or worse because there couldn't have been a worse time in our marriage.

In order for this marriage to work, we decided as a couple to go to grief counseling together. My logic for doing this was that it would help my husband to understand the pain I was going through and vice versa. To be honest, I couldn't focus on how he felt. I was overwhelmed with my own emotions. How does one walk out of a volcano of emotions?

During couple's counseling, I received individual counseling as well. We went to counseling for months to help each through this process. I needed him to be OK with the decision to stand by me through this journey because it wouldn't be an easy process. For example, I love playing blackjack when we go to Las Vegas. In life, you will be dealt a bad hand from time to time. The key to any bad hand is to know when to get up before you lose everything. I got up and fought for my marriage before I lost my husband. It was totally worth it.

For years, my husband put his feelings aside to tend to my every need throughout my grieving process. He has always made sure I was OK. That is his nature as husband, provider, and protector. For thirty years, he was a construction worker. His specialty is building or fixing things. I was the one thing he couldn't fix. Mr. Fix-it couldn't fix his wife.

I felt guilty at times because I couldn't reciprocate his emotions. I would often buy him material things as a sign of my affection. Three years into the journey I knew we couldn't keep living as we were. We had to figure this out this marriage situation one way or another. This turmoil was too much for me to bear at times. I felt overwhelmed daily and like a thousand bricks were on my shoulders. I made a conscious decision to recommit to my marriage. It was very hard at first, but we knew it was what we both wanted and needed.

Life will always throw obstacles your way, but it is how you handle situations together that represent a true testimony. When I lost my faith in God, myself, and my marriage, my husband would drop to his knees, pray for me, and ask God to give me the strength and courage to hear God again and renew my faith in the Lord.

It was very hard for me to believe in anything anymore. Growing up in a household where my God was the Almighty answered all prayers, I felt alone because he didn't answers my prayers. I couldn't or wouldn't believe the God I serves was so cruel that he brought this storm into my life that darn near destroyed me and definitely almost killed me.

I couldn't believe that God was that cruel. Hebrews 13:5 says, "I would never leave you or forsake you." I read that scripture over and over, yet it was still hard to believe. I would scream aloud, "Why, God? Why me? Help me, God! I can't bear the pain! My life is empty now, Lord. This loss is too much to bear. Help me, Lord!"

All I did was cry. My eyes were swollen from my tears that flowed every day. My heart was broken, and I didn't know how to fix it.

"Why, God? Why me?"

Night after night we lay next to one another, sexless, no cuddling, and or we barely kissed—not because my husband wouldn't jump at the first chance but because of my state of mind in dealing with grief. I just wasn't there in the relationship physically or mentally, as though I were having an out-of-body experience every day. I believed if I kissed my husband he would think or expect it would to lead to intimacy. That just wasn't happening in my world at that time. My husband eventually understood that I wasn't going to be intimate with him until I was truly ready.

So after about year, some much-needed intimacy resurfaced in our marriage. I thank God for my husband's patience, understanding, and honesty. I know it wasn't an easy journey, but the reward at the end was better than any money or trophy you could ever get in life. Being patient is not always easy, but the journey is well worth it. I have so much respect for my boo thang. His gentle and kind heart shines through the storm even amidst his own pain.

Men are taught early on not to show emotion or they will look weak, but even Jesus wept.

Jesus wept. John 11:35

MY HUSBAND'S PERSPECTIVE

Having a fine cigar and a glass of Patron on the rocks are the little things that used to give me relaxation and a peace of mind. Preserving moments like this would be few and far between in our home for a long time. That was my reality. As a construction worker by trade, working alongside my father, who brought me into the union, taught me many skills. But the best skill of all is that he taught me how to be a man. This is one of the greatest legacies a father can render to a son.

There were many days that turned into years of father-and-son talks that themselves were life lessons. I saw my father love my mother unconditionally. He treated her like the queen she is and never lost his dignity as the head of his household, a great provider, and a protector of his family. His faith and his love for God found him taking his family to church every Sunday to get the word of God and praise the Lord. My father used say to me we were blessed as a family.

If I could be half the man that my father was, it would be like looking in a mirror and stepping into an arena of greatness. My father talked to me as he usually did about life lessons while we were fishing. One day he said to me, "Son, if you find a woman that captures your heart and she loves you and treats you the way you supposed to treated, marry her."

He who findeth a wife finds a good thing. Proverbs 18:22

Teaching me about life lessons is what I admired most about my dad.

I experienced my first traumatic experience of loss when my father died when I was in my thirties. I was devastated about his death. I couldn't cope; my best friend was gone. The person whom I had looked up to and who taught me about life was no longer. My hero was gone.

But I remembered him telling me that if I found a great woman to make her my wife, and that's exactly what I did. I married my queen. She was everything my father and I talked about all those years: beautiful, intelligent, and with a little bit of sass!

My ride-or-die chick.

Then there was that night, and the phone rang late. That call changed our lives forever. The moment we got that phone call that Tre' had been shot, my heart starting beating fast.

I looked to my wife as we were lying in bed. We sprang up, rushed to get dressed, and headed to the hospital. I remember my wife stopping me in the truck to ask me to pray. We held hands and prayed. I saw the look of concern for her son on her face. We were so scared.

We got the hospital around 1 a.m., where our family greeted us at the door. It was a waiting game from there on. Our son was in surgery. We sat in the ER for hours waiting on some or any word for Tre'. Five hours had passed and still no word.

You know they say no news is good news, and we were all clinging to the hope of that. This would be the calm before the storm.

In the sixth hour, the doctors come out to get us. I grabbed my wife's hand, and we walked behind the police into a room where the doctor and nurses awaited us. We both were confused about why we weren't going to see our son. My wife was getting agitated and wanted to go see him. The doctor said, "I am so sorry, but your son didn't make it." And those words would forever define the life as we used to know it. My wife let out this loud piercing scream that rang out through the walls of the ER and fainted; I sprang into action and never stopped from that day on.

Getting my wife awake and making sure she was OK was my first concern. When she was conscious, she asked me, "What did the doctor say?

I had to repeat it her: "Tre' is dead."

She said, "No. I don't believe you. He can't be."

I needed to see him. I had to go with my wife to identify our son in the morgue. This had to be the second-worst day of my life. After we identified our son, we went back into the ER to inform our family that it was our son, and this would now be our reality. Everyone wanted to come back to our house, but I told them that my wife needed some time and space to process the loss of our son. So I told them she needed her sisters and mother right now.

Once we were home, I remember my wife going upstairs to take a shower, but I had to go upstairs to get her out of the water. The water was so hot; I thought she was going to scald herself. She was sobbing so hard in the shower. We both fell to our knees and embraced; we cried, cried, cried. Our hearts were broken. The family we had was no more. I put my wife in bed so she could rest. She was in a fog. I was walking around in circles pacing the floor. I dropped to my knees and prayed to my God, "Why, God? Why, God? Why, God?"

And he settled his countenance stedfastly, until he was ashamed and the man of God wept. 2 Kings 8:11

In the days ahead, my wife said she couldn't stay in our home anymore, so I decided to take her to a hotel to help with her anxiety. At least there we could stop and collect our thoughts as we planned our son's funeral. We had lots of visitors that daily came to our home or called to send their heartfelt condolences to my wife and me. The response was so overwhelming that I couldn't breathe at times. The air was so thick around me. I was running on adrenaline because I really couldn't sleep. We were grieving.

I felt helpless that I couldn't help my wife. Every day we would greet guests at our home and then return to the hotel to rest. Feeling exhausted, one night I drifted off into a deep sleep only to be awakened by a visitor, an angel, Tre'.

I said to him, "Tre'! Oh, my God!"

He said, "Mr. John, it's me. I need you to tell my mom I am OK, and I love her. I see her crying over me. I can't go to her because her heart is broken. Tell her I am with Mama!!" Then he told me, "Take care of my mom, Mr. John. She needs you." And then he disappeared.

I jumped up with tears running down my face. I sat on the side of the bed. I looked over at my wife, who was sleeping so peacefully, I didn't want to disturb her. So I patiently waited for her until she woke up. She saw the tears in my eyes and asked me what was wrong. I had to tell her I had a visit from our son. I proceeded to tell her what Tre' wanted her to know. She broke down in tears.

Jesus, fix it!

This wasn't the first time I was visited by an angel. Earlier in our relationship when my wife and I were engaged and planning our wedding, her grandmother came to me in my sleep and said, "You are good for my family," and then she kissed me on my forehead. Mind you, I never met Big Momma. I only heard great and funny stories about her. The morning I told my then-fiancé what I had experienced, her words were, "I am not surprised because I was her favorite." My wife always speaks highly of her grandmother and would often joke with me that if she were alive, I would be her favorite, which would knock out her spot as the favorite grandchild.

We had the funeral, and it was a beautiful celebration of life service for our son. We were physically, emotionally, and mentally drained. I felt like a squeezed lemon with no juice left. I decided that I needed to take my wife away so she could grieve in peace. We went to the Poconos, the first of many places we went to escape our reality. For four months we ran away from our house. It was no longer a home for us. Everyone wanted our story, and I was trying to protect my wife. She wasn't ready. My first priority was to take care of my wife because she was not doing well and wanted take her own life.

My heart was already broken into a million pieces, but seeing her like that broke my heart into a billion pieces. My wife was grieving over her only child, and there was nothing I could do for her. I was angry as hell because somebody destroyed my family. Our whole world was blown up. I couldn't even focus on myself right now because my wife needed me.

I decided to call a counselor for us because my wife was getting more and more depressed as time went on. She was barely eating, and we couldn't sleep.

Meanwhile, our son's death lit a fire in the community to do something about the gun violence in our city. We were contacted to do the marches and the rallies. They wanted my wife to speak out in the community. Something awoke in her. She was ready to fight for justice and his legacy and against the violence in the community. I thought she was taking on too much too fast, but I couldn't stop her. Her emotions were on a roller coaster. I often waited to see what type of mood she was in just to approach her about our day-to-day life stuff. She would lash out at me, and I just took it because I knew it wasn't her normally. She was grieving, and I felt helpless. All I could do was be there for her.

I was broken! While our life had changed, we couldn't fathom how to wrap our heads around how our life had forever changed.

After thirty years of construction, I decided to retire to be by my wife's side during this difficult time. She needed me, and I needed her. This vibrant, energetic woman with a beautiful smile and those dimples that lit a room up was no longer. The storm had hit our house and destroyed her. Sometimes I had to make decisions in the best interests of the family. She wasn't doing well, and I was afraid of losing her too. Months passed by, but things remained the same. Months turned into a year, and then another year. By the third year I felt like life had passed us by, yet we were stuck in the very first year after we lost our son.

Eventually, my wife threw herself into honoring his legacy. As for our marriage, she was sailing that ship. I had to be very patient. I felt neglected at times, but what's a guy to do but take care of his queen mentally and physically? I remember sitting on the side of the bed one morning, and after three long years of going and going, I broke down. I was that man who cried in the dark.

I told my wife he was my son too, and I was grieving as well. But I really couldn't grieve because she was grieving, and I had to be strong for her. For the first time in a long time I felt my wife reach out again to hold me. She wiped the tears from my eyes and said we would get through this together. The worst had happened to us.

In that moment, I had hope, keeping the faith that our marriage would survive the storm. It wasn't easy! It was all worth it in the end, and well worth the wait. I prayed a lot, and now my prayers were being answered.

I would read the bible regularly. Certain scriptures stuck out to me that I would say daily as we went through our lives. Keeping the faith was all I had to lean on. God was my refuge. The days weren't easy, sometimes even a struggle. Patience is a virtue.

I have my wife back now, with a little more sass and a new normal with a purpose. She is different now, and I know that. Grieving is a journey for us, and that journey will last a lifetime.

Is it perfect? No, there are times even now when she so consumed with other stuff or things it tends to overwhelm her. It took a while, but our communication has definitely gotten better through our journey. I can now sit her down and communicate to her that she needs a break when I feel she is overwhelmed. I always let her know I am here for her to help and will support her with everything she needs. A new normal is where we are at this time in our life, but we find our way one day at a time. Our date night became a new norm in our household.

Grief can destroy you as a man if you let it. It can put you onto a spiraling path that could be destructive rather than productive. But God, God sees all and knows all.

Endurance develops strength of character, and character strengthens our confident hope of salvation. Romans 5:4

We know the bible tells us that where there is life we will experience death. God made the heavens and the earth. The last thing that is said by the pastor before they lower the casket in the ground is "ashes to ashes, dust to dust."

Blessed are those who mourn, for they shall be comforted. Matthew 5:4

Your life is altered; your heart will be in pieces until you find your peace in your own time. Grief doesn't really have a time table. You will go through the appropriate grief steps in no particular order. Go through the stages, and get help from a professional. Find a support group to help you through journey.

Be careful what you think your thoughts tend run your life. Proverbs 4:23

Surround yourself with things that inspire you to be happy. You must find a new route to happiness. Oprah Winfrey said "Nature is the greatest spiritual teacher." Time waits on no one. Life will pass you by, and when you look up you won't remember anything you did because you were stagnant. You were stuck in a time zone that wouldn't allow you to move forward.

Self-care is mandatory. Find something of interest like meditation, yoga, a massage, or a walk in the park. Whatever it is you decide to do, let it be because it will bring you a sense of peace for the moment.

Fight for your life. Journal your thoughts and feelings; this will allow you to be honest with yourself and the people around you. Pain and love are connected. Let your pain serve as an inspiration to honor your loved ones. Let it be how you remember your loved ones.

Albert Einstein said, "Peace cannot be kept by force: It can only be achieved by understanding."

Hope is scary. Hope opens you to healing. It forces you to keep moving on because you really don't have a choice. You will experience tears. Along the way and out of nowhere, something will trigger a memory of your loved one. Cry your tears because it's part of the journey. You will remember a happy moment of your loved one and smile because you just want to freeze the moment forever. Being happy is not betrayal; being happy means moving on but keeping them in your heart forever.

Casting all your care upon him: for he careth for you. 1Peter 5:7

Chapter 7:

❖

7 Important Lessons I Have Learned

The loss of a child is excruciating. Most people, even close family members, cannot fully understand what parents go through spiritually, emotionally, and physically. Instead of advising parents at such a time, empathizing with them will always have a better impact. Generally, parents live with the void due to their child's loss for their entire life, and each day becomes a battle with their own life when they think about their child and the happiness they had because of the child. After going through a lot of turmoil, I have compiled a list of seven lessons that life has taught me after losing my son.

1. LOVE IS IMMORTAL

You will continue loving your child always; there will never be a moment in your life where you do not think about them. There is an unconditional love for children in the hearts of parents who long to talk to their children just like how it would be if the child were alive.

However, not many people talk about their dead children, as it still unfairly remains a taboo in society. Although talking about a lost child might not go down well in society, it does not stop parents from thinking about their children, saying their names, or talking about them. Just because it is awkward for some other person, parents who have lost a child cannot stop talking about their child because they love their children in life and beyond.

Love is patient, love is kind. It does not envy, it does not boast, it is not proud. It does not dishonor others, it is not self-seeking, it is not easily angered, it keeps no record of wrongs. Love does not delight in evil but rejoices with the truth. It always protects, always trusts, always hopes, always perseveres. Love never fails. But where there are prophecies, they will cease; where there are tongues, they will be stilled; where there is knowledge, it will pass away. 1 Corinthians 13:4-8

2. AN UNSPOKEN BOND EXISTS AMONG BEREAVED PARENTS

Ever since I lost my child, I have shared a strong bond with other bereaved parents. They all start by suddenly being kind, and we get connected through our hearts even if we have not known each other for long. Despite the circumstances and any shortcomings, bereaved parents bond better as they have gone through the agonizing experience, and it has left a void for life. Unfortunately, only people who have gone through this misery will be able to understand the pain from within of losing a child. The love for one's child never ceases for every bereaved parent.

3. The Grief Can Last a Lifetime

Parents will never be able to overcome the grief regardless of what they do, and there is no solution for this. The grief remains for life. There will be constant moments of extreme sadness, love, compassion, and helplessness, and there is no way out. Every bereaved parent will think about how the situation would have been different if their child were still alive. We often think about how they would look and how life would be perfect. The grief that comes with the loss of a child is inseparable, unforgettable, and stays with parents till their last breath. The parents will never stop thinking about the child even for a moment. With every passing day in life, parents only miss their child more, and you will start realizing that you will always love them unconditionally. Right from their child's first day at school, missed birthdays, holidays, and the wonderful moments they have had together will never come back no matter what, thus scarring such parents for a lifetime.

The pain tends to exist always. There is no escape from it, and you will realize that every single day without your child is a painful experience.

4. You Do Not Wish to Become a Part of This Club!

There is a Child Loss Club. This might actually sound strange to hear, but it is the only safe haven where most bereaved parents can somehow make peace with their loss. Everybody here only wishes to change the past so that they can have their child alive to hug again.

After a few sessions with these kindred souls, you will realize that you are all compassionately grounded, loving healers and beautiful souls actually helping one another in ways you would not typically have imagined. By listening to the experiences of loss, you realize how incredibly strong people can be. We display a bold face even when we are breaking down.

Parents who have lost their children at a young age do their best to honor their children's memory. They fight against everything possible to make sure that the loss of their child is not left without any action. Their only purpose is to try their best that no parent ever goes through the ordeal that they have gone through. To know what it is to lose in life, you definitely have to hang out with this club at least once, and you will realize that the loss of their child is the pain that fuels their fight. The way they channel their sadness, frustration, and helplessness into a cause to try to ensure that what happened to their child does not happen to anyone else is amazing.

Love is irreplaceable and unconditional; it exists beyond life, and once you love someone, you love them for life. To understand what it is to love unconditionally, you definitely have to talk to a bereaved parent. You'll know that there is nothing beyond pure love.

5. The Emptiness Stays Forever

No matter what you look at, the chair, the room, the bed, or the family picture, it all starts looking empty. You will realize that there are a lot more empty places in your house than you had thought. The gap created in our lives can never be filled, and even with time, the scars never heal. Even if friends and relatives continuously advise you to move on or stop thinking about your child, those words never make sense anymore. You will continue to miss your child, and you know that they will never be back no matter what you do. Your broken heart, the pain, and the traumatic experience continue.

This lasts for a lifetime. We continue to miss them, and it would be great if people stopped asking bereaved parents to move on.

6. Holidays Are Never the Same Again

Do you know how holidays become dreadful for parents without their child? No matter how many years later, the void still remains, and the bereaved parents will hit bottom imagining how precious their child was and how badly they need them on a holiday. Parents think that losing their organs or a leg would be better any day rather than losing a child. They would trade all that they have to get their child back. Holidays become too hard for bereaved parents. You cannot put yourself in their shoes. So, don't try understanding. Just continue to support them in all possible ways, and that would be the greatest help you can ever do.

7. With Sorrow, You Also Realize There Are Joyous Moments

Although parents continue to be in grief for the loss of their child, it does not mean that they lack happiness. They accept the fact that their child is not with them anymore and still have a few joyous moments. They become more intense with their feelings. With more grief, they are also able to experience more joy.

They believe that they have gone through unimaginable pain, so they can also go through unimaginable happiness whenever they can. They stop being materialistic and start taking life the way it unfolds, rather than being depressed or trying to fight about something that can never be fixed. Things that did not seem otherwise will never be taken for granted. Overall, bereaved parents start feeling joyous, and they accept the reality of their lives as their new normal.

Although the child is no more, being their parent is the best gift that life could ever give them.

That gift is inseparable even by death. The Ghost of Christmas past.

When the child was with us, there was magic in life, and every moment was joyous. Each smile was so beautiful, with endless possibilities that reflected from its shine.

Christmas was the best time for the child, just like how he wanted it to be. He might have known that the number of Christmas memories he has will not be many. He was there with us for a few years, yet gave us so many memories to live with!

The Christmases we shared were so perfect with such beautiful days and such unexpected little moments of joy that sometimes it makes us feel that the world is a beautiful place to live in with so much love all around.

We create memories with our children with the movies we take them to, the weekend outings in the park, or the home-cooked dinner made with love and affection, resulting in a memorable meal. It was all fun, always, when the child was there. But it all resulted in a void now, something irreplaceable and inconsolable. All the best things we had in life are gone: the smile, the affection, the simplicity in the eyes of the child; we have it captured in our hearts.

He is not here anymore! Still, I try to imagine him every year, celebrating his birthday and calling out for his mom. While everyone else asks me to move on and lead my life with joy, how can I? With the apple of my eyes gone, every day seems to be a fight.

The enthusiasm that exists in life is gone. I do not wish to indulge in any activity anymore or talk much. Sometimes I just hope that my child is back in my arms where I feel he belongs. His death still seems like a long dream that just won't end.

I am grateful to the people who have supported us always, who gave us the required support and time to ourselves to help us heal. I know that they still see the pain in our eyes when they think about our loss. The only purpose I have when I wake up every day is to live one more day without my beloved child. No matter what religious beliefs indicate, I attain my salvation by living my life daily, somehow enduring the loss of my son for another one of many days to come. The hole in my heart is always aching for my son and, no matter how much I try to forget about it, the memory never seems to fade. I know Tre' would want me to be happy even now. Some semblance of happiness is what I must strive for daily from the moment I wake up.

The depression I suffered was beyond comprehension, reason, or justification. I completely gave up trying to make sense of Tre's untimely death and the tremendous weight of the loss.

The loss of a child changes the lives of parents in ways that can neither be expressed nor ignored. The suddenness? The shock? The sadness? I know that Tre' would never want us to be sad. He was joyous, upbeat, and smiling for the entirety of his short life. He would not tolerate a pity party.

No. I would have to take it up as a challenge to go on with life and at least seek light at the end of the tunnel. Perhaps then I would be able to live on my own new terms. I doubted that I could ever be happy again. Would I ever again spread happiness the way that Tre' had? Losing my baby boy could never be fixed. I knew this intellectually. But I was beginning to wonder, to hope, that I would fulfil a purpose and that Tre' had not died in vain.

Chapter 8:

— ❖ —

Get Help

In our society, we often look at sitting on a shrink's couch like a taboo and say, "That's not for me." When my son died, I knew I had to get help, or I wouldn't be here and alive to share my story. Getting help can save your life. Grief can be overwhelming. Depression starts to set in, and your days turn darker than any shade of black you have seen.

There are numerous advantages to getting counseling. For example, you are able to talk about your loved one openly with no inhibitions or judgments. Tears will flow, and even laughter will appear as you remember all the memories you shared with that person, thus keeping them alive in your heart.

This is one of the reasons I love counseling. It introduces you to a new world of thinking by a trained, objective professional. Sometimes we need conversations outside of our friends and family. We can show a greater side of vulnerability. We need to talk with someone who can dig deep inside our emotions to help us work out the malfunctioning kinks.

Grieving parents may say to themselves, "My child died because I was wrong." Sometimes a parent may feel like the death of their child is their own fault. Some couples even divorce over grief-related issues. In life, there are numerous would-haves and could-haves. We have to literally train our mind to focus on what we are working with today. You are still alive and capable. Counseling is so instrumental in situations like this. It can even help a marriage between two willing adults. I know it tremendously helped my marriage. Personally, it allowed me to exhale.

Oftentimes we really don't have a choice except to go on with our life to maintain our daily living. Yes, it was very hard for me at first. I felt everyone went about their life, and I was still stuck in the same grievous place, time, and day that my son was killed.

Within the stages of grief (denial, anger, bargaining, depression, and acceptance), there is a different timeline for every individual. When healing is unhealthy, some people stay in a zone for ten or twenty years. This doesn't allow them to cope and move forward in any area of life. Some refuse. Some may always refer to their loved one as though they were still in the earthly realm.

What do I mean by unhealthy healing? Let's say that an individual has broken a toe and the bone heals, but it is still slightly crooked. After eight weeks, that person may not feel pain anymore as they walk. Things appear to be normal on the surface. But perhaps when they put on a pair of shoes with heels, their toe still hurts because the bone healed improperly. Grieving can be the same and be coupled with improper healing. Counseling helped me and my husband get through the stages of grieving in a healthier manner in our own time. To survive, we had to do the work conducive to healing. This is a full time-effort requiring your undivided attention.

After the loss of a loved one, we all know that the rent, mortgage, or light bill has to be paid. These businesses are preoccupied with making money, and empathy is not on their list. I was very fortunate because I had a job that allowed me to take a whole year off to focus solely on me. I went to counseling weekly until I started to feel stronger.

You must do what is best for you. No one can tell you how you feel or when you are ready to return to work. Talk to a counselor or your pastor; find a local grief counseling service to support you, or just talk to a friend. Keeping your feelings all bottled up will only make them fester in the different stages of grief.

Keeping my faith throughout the storm help me get through it. Pray and pray often. Thank you, Father, for the faith of those in my family who went before me and who first put my feet on the path to knowing you. I confess that I cannot see you or touch you or hear you (maybe sometimes I hear you in the form of my conscious), but I know you are there. The evidence of your love and care for me is just too strong to be discounted.

Thank you heavenly father for my faith, without it in my life I would be a lost soul. Lord, continue to give me the strength and wisdom to know you better, because of you, I know I am blessed and highly favored.

All in all, I have learned to encourage myself and appreciate the benefits of counseling. It aids me in managing those ranging emotions. Don't knock it until you have tried it because it can enrich your life if you let it.

The counsel of the Lord standeth for ever, the thoughts of his heart to all generations. Psalms 33:11

Chapter 9:

— ❖ —

Honor Your Loved One

Honoring your loved one is a medicinal and gentle way to manage your emotions. It takes some of the abrasiveness out of grieving.

Additionally, creating grief rituals can help us maintain a connection with our loved ones in loving, healing ways that provide us with a sense of peace. This process is for you as well to maintain the memory of your beloved. This is a great way to encourage ourselves. Let the pain be your inspiration. Let the healing process begin. The process of honoring your loved one lends itself to keeping your loved one alive in your heart, mind, and way of life.

Now may the Lord of peace himself give you peace at all times and in every way. The Lord be with all of you. 2Thessalonians 3:16

First, remember who your loved one was and what they loved and enjoyed. Let that be your starting point for your re-membrance. For me, it meant honoring my son's legacy with a foundation or recognizing his love of basketball with a tournament. But you may not want to do something on that grand a scale. Start simple and small. For example, plant a tree in honor of them, or put a plaque on a bench in their favorite park, with the park's permission, of course.

I have talked to others who have experienced loss, and they have given financial scholarships in their loved one's name to the high school they attended. The scholarship was given to a graduating senior going to college. You can also do a 5K walk or run to raise money for a particular charity. It doesn't matter what you do to honor your loved one as long as you do it. Make your pain be your purpose and your struggles your strength. I did.

During this time in my life and as I walk on new ground, I have learned and absorbed so much. Listed below are some constructive ideas that I found while perusing a number of websites and books. There are lots of resources out there. Here are a few ideas.

1. Charity Drives. Set up a drive for a charity close to your heart and your loved one's heart. It could be helping the organizations that aided you while your loved one was sick, or it could be helping in a different way. For example, if your loved one were a veteran, organize a food drive to help homeless veterans get a hot meal; if your loved one were a teacher, help underprivileged kids get toys for Christmas. Just think about what your loved one did or was passionate about and choose something that is an extension of this.

2. Memorialize Them. There are a variety of different options for this, and you could do something personal such as visiting a favorite spot each day, month, or year that you used to frequent, turning their old clothes into a quilt or stuffed animal, creating a collage of your favorite pictures, and even having their ashes turned into fireworks or jewelry.

3. Talk to Others. Don't shy away from the memories of your loved one. Talk to others about them, and share stories and anecdotes. You never know how hearing of this can help others, and this would be an excellent way of keeping your loved one and their knowledge alive, particularly if their story were brave or moving and could inspire others.

4. Finish Something for Them. Rarely do we have everything tied in a bow neatly before we die, and there is usually something on their "list" that they wanted to do or were in the middle of completing. Finishing it can be a catharsis for you as well as an honoring of their memory.

5. Plant a Tree. Planting trees or flowers can be an excellent way to honor a memory and gives you something to look at as a reminder in years to come. When flowers bloom each season, it's a beautiful way to remember, or sometimes sitting by the specific tree you planted can make you feel closer to them.

Here is a list of suggestions for remembrances.

1. Buy a special candle and light it at times that are special to your loved one's memory, such as a birthday, Mother's/Father's Day, and anniversaries. Light one at your dinner table as a reminder of your loved one's presence at holiday gatherings.

2. Write special notes and put them inside balloons; fill them with helium and have a "releasing" gathering to let them go.

3. Create an altar of remembrance to keep in your home as a space for you to spend time with your loved one. It can be on a shelf or small accent table, just for holidays/birthdays, or as a permanent fixture.

4. Create a scrapbook of memories and photos. You can even create a digital scrapbook with a blog or website to remember your loved one by.

5. On birthdays, holidays, anniversaries, and the like, buy your loved one a gift (or re-gift some of their gently used belongings you don't mind parting with) and donate to a local hospital, nursing home, shelter, or someone in need.

6. Hang up Christmas stockings for a loved one and have everyone write a special note to put inside.

7. Find a tree in the canyons or woods, tie a colored ribbon around it, and go frequently to remember your loved one. (This can be especially helpful when ashes have been scattered and there may be no grave site.)

8. Have a party to honor your loved one on their birthday.

9. Offer a charitable donation (monetary or in-kind) or a scholarship in a loved one's name.

10. Frame a piece of clothing or create a shadow box with special items that remind you of your loved one.

11. Plant a strong, healthy tree, rosebush, or whatever may have special meaning to you. You can even dedicate an herb garden or flower bed in their name. Then you can foster your connection to your loved one as you care for your beautiful plant.

12. Buy a holiday ornament each year to remember your loved one.

13. If you go on a trip at a special anniversary time, do something special to remember your loved one on the trip,

such as tossing a rose into the ocean or lighting a candle.

14. Have a loved one's ring made into a new setting for a necklace or other jewelry.

15. Let bubbles go with a reflection or special wish to send to the loved one.

16. Host a "family memory" evening where you share pictures, reminisce about special times, and create a scrapbook/box of memories.

17. Bake cookies or other treats together, and take them to someone who is sick or unable to get out this time of year.

18. Decorate a small tree and take it to a hospital or nursing home for a patient who may need some extra warmth.

19. Create a memory quilt or stuffed animal using photos or clothing items from your loved one to cuddle up with.

20. Start a collection of stories, poems, or quotes about the season. Place them in a book that honors your loved one, and add to these each year.

21. Attend an event that reminds you of your loved one, such as a sporting event, concert, play, or movie.

22. Visit your loved one's gravesite and bring them flowers, letters, balloons, or something meaningful to you, such as toy cars for a car lover.

23. Participate in a charity event such as a race or walk, help feed the hungry at Thanksgiving, or start a drive to benefit a local organization by collecting food, books, or stuffed animals.

24. Create a remembrance wreath ritual with your family at a particular time each year.

25. Have a watch engraved with your loved one's name, or carry a locket with a photo to remember them always.

26. Design it yourself! Design a special ritual all of your own. Remember, all that's important is that it is meaningful to you.

I have come to understand that not all situations are created equal. Healthy healing is a process. Perhaps you may want to consider counseling before you can truly honor your loved one. We are human and have to deal with intricate issues of the heart. Now that I am better and healthier, I can use my remaining energy to honor my beloved son with every fiber of my being. I am committed to this cause and his legacy for the rest of my life through The Tre' Devon Lane Foundation. (tdlane.org)

May the God of hope fill you with all joy and peace as you trust in him, so that you may overflow with hope by the power of the Holy Spirit. Romans 15:13

To truly honor those we have lost is to embrace living again.

Chapter 10:

— ❖ —

The New Normal

"The reality is that you will grieve forever. You will not get over the loss of a loved one; you learn to live with it. You will heal, and you will rebuild yourself around the loss you have suffered. You will be whole again, but you will never be the same," says Elisabeth Kubler-Ross.

It's time to reflect on my journey from the very beginning to where I am today. As we know, grieving comes in all forms such as a loss of a loved one, a divorce, loss of a home, loss of a job, or even loss of a pet. I also learned that pain comes in all flavors and can change the complexion of life. It reminds me of the unpredictable, volatile waves of an ocean. One day the waves and tides are riding high, and on another day the waters are still yet running deep. Putting the grief and pain in perspective can be challenging at first, but it will come in your own time. You will find your way emotionally back home.

Anxiety weighs down the heart, but a kind word cheers it up. Proverbs 12:25

Like a thief in the night, just like that my joy was stolen in a multiplicity of ways. I want to convey the totality of losing a loved one. It encompasses not only losing the loved one but also the unexpected and brutal halt of losing wonderful experiences with that individual. The graduation from college, the first grandchild, the wedding, the first car or job will never transpire and have evaporated into thin air. It could simply be the daily, "I love you, Mom," or a hug and kiss on the cheek that brought you joy and satisfaction in life. Now there are no more beautiful memories to create.

Situations of this caliber can cut and penetrate the deepest level of one's being. Someone who loved me more than anyone on earth is gone in less than sixty seconds, and no one can replace him. Some people in this situation can have another baby, but it will never take the place of that individual, and life will never be quite the same.

I remember my grief counselor saying to me, "You are going to have a new normal."

I responded, "What does that look like?"

She said, "Life without your son. But you never forget him because you will always have him with you in your heart and all of the wonderful memories."

I asked myself, *How could this be? My life is forever changed. I will never be able to tell my son I love him or give him a hug. I have now lost the ability to create more wonderful memories together.*

"Lord, help me," I prayed. "I don't know if I can do this journey."

He gives power to the faint, and to them that have no might he increases strength. Isaiah 40:29

I spent the first three years in a place and space where black raindrops fell. When my son left this dimension, the sun in the sky wasn't as bright, the grass wasn't as green, and the sky was perpetually gray. Food didn't even taste the same, and some days it just didn't matter any longer. I emotionally bled, experienced a hundred shades of pain, and cried with and without tears. At times, I did not want to live. How was I going process and cope with this devastating loss to our family? I felt alone, even though I was not. I have my husband and family for support. I just felt the need to walk alone for the first part of this journey.

Grieving has a selfish component. It is demanding and consumes all of your strength and focus. When you are in the throes of grief, you can only see and feel your pain. This has a tendency to shut out others. During the apex of grief, one is self-absorbed. If grief could talk, it would say, "I don't hear you. I don't see you. I am hurting and only see my pain." The end result is me, me, and me. This is not intentional or malicious. However, to remain in this state is toxic, has blinding effects, and hurts others.

Initially, in my new normal, I was very angry, and it was laced with bitterness. I lashed out at my husband constantly. I knew it wasn't him, but because he was the closest thing to me, I took my anger out on him. He had to reach deeply beyond the pain to help me while he was still hurting.

Life as I knew it before was history. I was a totally different person. I felt like I had my guard up at all times. For example, I was jumpy when I heard gunfire on television. I have been traumatized by the mere mention of gun violence. I have diagnosed myself as having PTSD, a mental health condition that's triggered by a terrifying event, experiencing it or witnessing it. Symptoms may include flashbacks, nightmares, and severe anxiety as well as uncontrollable thoughts about the event. You can't even turn on the news without hearing reports of several shootings around the country or even the world. My heart aches and bleeds for these families.

Let's carefully look at the condition as it relates to my life. I experienced a terrifying event, check. I experienced it first-hand, check. I have flashbacks, check, and nightmares, check, and anxiety, check. Yes, I would say I have PTSD. My life has changed forever. After a tragedy or a devastating loss, most people will have some type of aftershock or triggered reaction that will surface.

Some people who have experienced what I did become and stay angry with God. This is usually reactionary and unproductive. For me, He has been my true source of help in this life-changing experience. He helped me turn my pain into one of my greatest victories. My personal best is yet to come.

When tragedy hits, you are walking in shock and numbness in the first year. The world stops, and your emotions have not caught up with the reality of the situation. When shock is in operation, there is a lot of crying. When reality sets in, there is a lot of misery. Around years two and three are the worst, the Band-Aid comes off; everything becomes real to you, and this hits you like a ton of bricks. The anxiety level is really kicking in during this time. The pain is brutal.

Casting all your care upon him: for he cares for you. 1 Peter 5:7

After the death of my son I did not celebrate a birthday for four years. I felt that if I reaped an ounce of happiness, I would feel guilty because my son wasn't here to share the joy with me.

Holidays have been hard. My suggestion to anyone in this situation is to do as much or as little as you want. Don't feel under pressure because it is the "season." My husband and I had a secret password, so when either one of us felt uncomfortable or overwhelmed we would just say the password. This means, "Get our coats, and let's go fast."

I love my family and all of their loyal support. They have upheld me. Until 2016, they wouldn't celebrate a Christmas out of respect for me. After four long years of not celebrating the Christmas season, I felt like I had to release my family, so I decided to have an "ugly sweater" party at my home and invite family and friends. The one thing they had to bring was an ornament for my son to put on the tree. I thought this was the best was way to include my son's memory in the festivities. Doing the party and hosting Christmas dinner was a lot, but it felt like a weight was lifted off my shoulders. But letting life pass me wasn't an option anymore. My life has been altered in many ways, and my heart is in pieces, but I must find a new route to my happiness.

I do a lot of reflecting about my life. The words echoed in my mind, "Where do I go from here?" I had an epiphany. We can't change the past; we can only allow God to see us through the rest of the journey. I can't change what happened, but I can extract solace out of my new normal by celebrating the legacy of my son through The Tre' Devon Lane Foundation. Our foundation wants to ignite change in the community by decreasing gun violence and developing solutions for empowerment.

My son was in college and died due to his heroic efforts by shielding two women from being shot. This is a testament to his character. His life counts. I am taking my life back and preserving the legacy of my son.

Today, I choose. I choose to breathe again by moving forward and upward. I cannot afford to look down into that abyss where despair, dread, and depression hold hands. I have moved from not wanting to live to just existing to living with purpose again. I am conscious, actively awake and in participation with life. As a result of what happened to my son, I was powerless and had no real control of it. We can't choose our battles, but we can choose our current actions. This is our power.

Charity suffereth long, and is kind; charity envieth not; charity vaunteth not itself, is not puffed up. Doth not behave itself unseemly, seeketh not her own, is not easily provoked, thinketh no evil. 1Corinthians 13:4–5

Now that I am in this new chapter of life, I am also committed to helping and enriching the lives of other mothers who have tragically lost loved ones. We are reaching out to mothers across this entire nation. I have fellowshipped with other mothers, and some days we have carried each other. Some days we give strength. Some days we receive strength. Praying became our norm.

Heavenly father, thank you for my grandmother who instilled in me earlier on in my life the importance of knowing you God. Although I cannot see you, or touch you, if I be still I can hear you. For I know you are real. Thank you father for my faith, without it in my life I would be a lost soul. Father God continue to give me strength and wisdom to know you better. God, my life is different, but I know you got me. Because I know you I am blessed and highly favored Amen.

Answer me when I call to you, O my righteous God. Give me relief from my distress; be merciful to me and hear my prayer. Psalm 4

As I steadily heal, I am working on a building called forgiveness. It's a work in progress. I am like a bird migrating in that direction. The healing process dictates that we explore new emotional ground where the foundation is healthy.

Forgiveness is a part of that process. I spoke to another lady who lost her fiancé over $35.00 and a pack of cigarettes due to gun violence. Gun violence is like an infectious disease spreading throughout America. It seems like before you can finish drinking a can of soda, someone else has been shot. There needs to be a paradigm shift in the minds of our youth. Who knows? We may have to take things to a subliminal level by, for example, initiating anti-gun classes within the educational system starting at four years old and up.

I am not the only one who has experienced a new normal. I have often contemplated the fact that I will never have any grandchildren. Honestly, this saddens me. A dear friend also lost her son to gun violence. In her new normal, she is raising the child of her son, her grandson. It has been quite challenging as she witnesses the uncanny similarities of her grandson to her son. He is just like his father.

I would like to share a Facebook post thought I wrote the night before I turned fifty.

"As I sit here on my couch, I am reflecting on my last night of my 40s. I got married, my son graduated high school and went to college, then he was tragically killed, and I found a new purpose. So I experienced happiness, joy, sadness, broken-heartedness, strength, courage, and resilience, all in one decade. God is good. I am truly grateful to begin a new chapter. For the first time I'm feeling excited about what the possibilities may hold for me."

The light may seem dim, but I know there is light at the end of the tunnel on the other side of this journey. I am even smiling more now. Keep the faith! Pray! God will hear your prayers.

But verily God hath heard me; he hath attended to the voice of my prayer. Psalms 66:19

My husband and I are dating again like it is the very first time we met because I am not the woman he used to know. Learning my triggers and being patient but, more important, being understanding is essential to reconnecting as a couple. We pray together; having God in our marriage gives us that foundation. Communication plays a key role, especially during the rebuilding of this ground work.

God puts people in your life for a reason or a season. My husband was placed in my life for this moment of the storm to support me through this difficult journey. I thought it was a short season with my son, but God had other plans for him; however, it was the best nineteen years of my life with my baby. Self-care is important for healing this is why we travel because it helps us escape from our reality. Do what you love; what makes you happy even if it is only for a short period of time. In between the pain you will still have joyous moments that will emerge because each day will be different.

Take this journey one day at time. Write down your thoughts and feelings in a journal. This will allow you to be open and honest with yourself and the people around you. I will fight for change and what I believe in to fulfill my purpose. I have decided to make a difference. Through my pain my purpose was birthed. One of my memorable moments was standing shoulder-to- shoulder with the democrats on state capitol steps in Washington, DC fighting for change. Taking a selfie with the new Governor Phil Murphy of New Jersey and his wife, Tammy, meeting Democratic Leader Nancy Pelosi and Senator Cory Booker, and meeting Congressman John Lewis, and meeting Gabby Gifford were just small parts of my new normal.

I am a survivor, and I will use my voice to share my story to help or save others. We are broken but blessed! Although we have been through a storm, we survived. Yes, we survive with a purpose. Always remember that no storm is too big when you have faith in God.

> **And the Lord, he it is that doth go before thee; he will be with thee, he will not fail thee, neither forsake thee: fear not, neither be dismayed. Deuteronomy 31:8**

Ideas and Tools for Grieving

People grieve in different ways. For some, we have experienced a traumatic loss, and most days, we tend to shut down and are not in the mood to talk to the others during this grieving process. Journaling our feelings and thoughts are a welcome substitution for talking. Losing a loved one is a life altering piece of the puzzle that will forever change your family circle or friendships. In this section of the book, you will be able to write down your thoughts and your feeling at the moment, which will allow you to reflect on your journey in the grieving process. Journaling can be therapeutic.

Emotional Word Wheel

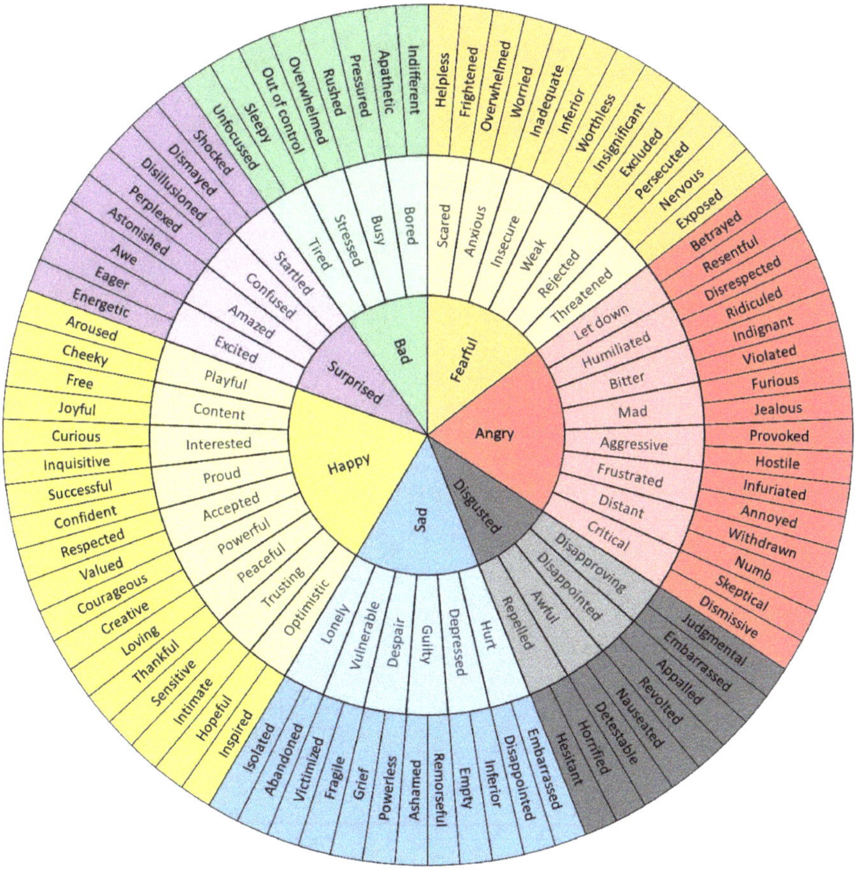

JOURNAL NOTES

_____

_____

_____

_____

_____

_____

_____

_____

_____

_____

_____

_____

JOURNAL NOTES

JOURNAL NOTES

_____

_____

_____

_____

_____

_____

_____

_____

_____

_____

_____

_____

JOURNAL NOTES

_____

_____

_____

_____

_____

_____

_____

_____

_____

_____

_____

_____

_____

JOURNAL NOTES

JOURNAL NOTES

_____

_____

_____

_____

_____

_____

_____

_____

_____

_____

_____

_____

JOURNAL NOTES

_____

_____

_____

_____

_____

_____

_____

_____

_____

_____

_____

_____

JOURNAL NOTES

JOURNAL NOTES

_____

_____

_____

_____

_____

_____

_____

_____

_____

_____

_____

_____

JOURNAL NOTES

_____

_____

_____

_____

_____

_____

_____

_____

_____

_____

_____

_____

JOURNAL NOTES

_____

_____

_____

_____

_____

_____

_____

_____

_____

_____

_____

_____

_____

JOURNAL NOTES

_____

_____

_____

_____

_____

_____

_____

_____

_____

_____

_____

_____

_____

JOURNAL NOTES

JOURNAL NOTES

_____

_____

_____

_____

_____

_____

_____

_____

_____

_____

_____

_____

_____

JOURNAL NOTES

_____

_____

_____

_____

_____

_____

_____

_____

_____

_____

_____

_____

_____

JOURNAL NOTES

_____

_____

_____

_____

_____

_____

_____

_____

_____

_____

_____

_____

_____

_____

JOURNAL NOTES

Important Hotline Numbers

Grief Recovery Helpline 1-800-445-4808

National Suicide Prevention Lifeline 1-800-273-8255

Parents of Murdered Children 1-888-818-7662

National Center for Post-Traumatic Stress
Disorder Info Line 1-802-296-6300

National Institute of Mental Health Depression &
Panic Disorder Hotline 1-800-421-4211

The Compassionate Friends Supporting Family
After a Child Dies 877 969-0010

National Alliance on Mental Illness 800-950-6264

References

A quote by Albert Einstein. (n.d.). Retrieved from https://www. goodreads.com/quotes/4464-peace-cannot-be-kept-by-force-it-can-only-be

A quote by Mahatma Gandhi. (n.d.). Retrieved from https://www. goodreads.com/quotes/24499-be-the-change-that-you-wish-to-see-in-the

Austingrief.org | The Austin Center for Grief & Loss. (n.d.). Retrieved from https://www.austingrief.org/

Bible Hub: Search, Read, Study the Bible in Many Languages. (n.d.). Retrieved from https://biblehub.com/

Foreword Poem, (n.d.). Retrieved from http://author unknown

Geoffrey Roberts www.facebook.com/thewhitehousechurch. (n.d.). Retrieved from Geoffrey Roberts www.facebook.com/ thewhitehousechurch website: http://Geoffrey Roberts www. facebook.com/thewhitehousechurch

Hotlines. (n.d.). Retrieved from https://griefresourcenetwork.com/ crisis-center/hotlines/

Imgur. (2015, March 15). Emotion Wheel. Retrieved from https:// imgur.com/a/CkxQC

Inspiringquotes.us. (n.d.). Elisabeth Kubler-Ross quote: The reality is that you will grieve forever. You will not "get over" the lo. Retrieved from https://www.inspiringquotes.us/quotes/5Laj_ RVYn7MfU

Kaiser, S. (n.d.). Internet Resources. Retrieved from http://skdesigns. com/internet/articles/prose/niebuhr/serenity_prayer/

"Nature is our greatest spiritual teacher." Oprah Winfrey. (2016, January 15). Retrieved from http://seasonedsingleness.com/ nature-is-our-greatest-spiritual-teacher-oprah-winfrey/

Sue. (2019, May 22). Serenity Prayer. Retrieved from http://www. allaboutprayer.org/serenity-prayer

The Compassionate Friends Non-Profit Organization for Grief. (n.d.). Retrieved from https://www.compassionatefriends.org/

"Growth is necessary for the progress in the journey." Regina Thompson-Jenkins. (2016).

CPSIA information can be obtained
at www.ICGtesting.com
Printed in the USA
LVHW080602100820
662780LV00008B/357